Date Paired	Cage No:	Cock No:	Variety		
				MW00946960	
	Date Laid	Date Hatched	Sex	Ring No:	Band Color
Chick 1					
Chick2					
Chick 3					
Chick4					
Chick 5					
Chick 6					
Chick 7					
Chick 8					
Chick 9					
Chick 10					

Notes

Date Paired	Cage No:	Cock No:	Variety	Hen No:	Variety
	Date Laid	Date Hatched	Sex	Ring No:	Band Color
Chick 1					
Chick2					
Chick 3					
Chick4					
Chick 5					
Chick 6					
Chick 7					
Chick 8					
Chick 9					
Chick 10					

Notes

Date Paired	Cage No:	Cock No:	Variety	Hen No:	Variety
	Date Laid	Date Hatched	Sex	Ring No:	Band Color
Chick 1					
Chick2					
Chick 3					
Chick4					
Chick 5					
Chick 6					
Chick 7					
Chick 8					
Chick 9					
Chick 10					

Notes

Date Paired	Cage No:	Cock No:	Variety	Hen No:	Variety
	Date Laid	Date Hatched	Sex	Ring No:	Band Color
Chick 1					
Chick2					
Chick 3					
Chick4					
Chick 5					
Chick 6					
Chick 7					
Chick 8					
Chick 9					
Chick 10					

Notes

Date Paired	Cage No:	Cock No:	Variety	Hen No:	Variety
	Date Laid	Date Hatched	Sex	Ring No:	Band Color
Chick 1					
Chick2					
Chick 3					
Chick4					
Chick 5					
Chick 6					
Chick 7					
Chick 8					
Chick 9					
Chick 10					

Notes

Date Paired	Cage No:	Cock No:	Variety	Hen No:	Variety
	Date Laid	Date Hatched	Sex	Ring No:	Band Color
Chick 1					
Chick2					
Chick 3					
Chick4					
Chick 5					
Chick 6					
Chick 7					
Chick 8					
Chick 9					
Chick 10					

Notes

Date Paired	Cage No:	Cock No:	Variety	Hen No:	Variety
	Date Laid	Date Hatched	Sex	Ring No:	Band Color
Chick 1					
Chick2					
Chick 3					
Chick4					
Chick 5					
Chick 6					
Chick 7					
Chick 8					
Chick 9					
Chick 10					

Notes

Date Paired	Cage No:	Cock No:	Variety	Hen No:	Variety
	Date Laid	Date Hatched	Sex	Ring No:	Band Color
Chick 1					
Chick2					
Chick 3					
Chick4					
Chick 5					
Chick 6					
Chick 7					
Chick 8					
Chick 9					
Chick 10					

Notes

Date Paired	Cage No:	Cock No:	Variety	Hen No:	Variety
	Date Laid	Date Hatched	Sex	Ring No:	Band Color
Chick 1					
Chick2					
Chick 3					
Chick4					
Chick 5					
Chick 6					
Chick 7					
Chick 8					
Chick 9					
Chick 10					

Notes

Date Paired	Cage No:	Cock No:	Variety	Hen No:	Variety
	Date Laid	Date Hatched	Sex	Ring No:	Band Color
Chick 1					
Chick2					
Chick 3					
Chick4					
Chick 5					
Chick 6					
Chick 7					
Chick 8					
Chick 9					
Chick 10					

Notes

Date Paired	Cage No:	Cock No:	Variety	Hen No:	Variety
	Date Laid	Date Hatched	Sex	Ring No:	Band Color
Chick 1					
Chick2					
Chick 3					
Chick4					
Chick 5					
Chick 6					
Chick 7					
Chick 8					
Chick 9					
Chick 10					

Notes

Date Paired	Cage No:	Cock No:	Variety	Hen No:	Variety
	Date Laid	Date Hatched	Sex	Ring No:	Band Color
Chick 1					
Chick2					
Chick 3					
Chick4					
Chick 5					
Chick 6					
Chick 7					
Chick 8					
Chick 9					
Chick 10					

Notes

Date Paired	Cage No:	Cock No:	Variety	Hen No:	Variety
	Date Laid	Date Hatched	Sex	Ring No:	Band Color
Chick 1					
Chick2					
Chick 3					
Chick4					
Chick 5					
Chick 6					
Chick 7					
Chick 8					
Chick 9					
Chick 10					

Notes

Date Paired	Cage No:	Cock No:	Variety	Hen No:	Variety
	Date Laid	Date Hatched	Sex	Ring No:	Band Color
Chick 1					
Chick2					
Chick 3					
Chick4					
Chick 5					
Chick 6					
Chick 7					
Chick 8					
Chick 9					
Chick 10					

Notes

Date Paired	Cage No:	Cock No:	Variety	Hen No:	Variety
	Date Laid	Date Hatched	Sex	Ring No:	Band Color
Chick 1					
Chick2					
Chick 3					
Chick4					
Chick 5					
Chick 6					
Chick 7					
Chick 8					
Chick 9					
Chick 10					

Notes

Date Paired	Cage No:	Cock No:	Variety	Hen No:	Variety
	Date Laid	Date Hatched	Sex	Ring No:	Band Color
Chick 1					
Chick2					
Chick 3					
Chick4					
Chick 5					
Chick 6					
Chick 7					
Chick 8					
Chick 9					
Chick 10					

Notes

Date Paired	Cage No:	Cock No:	Variety	Hen No:	Variety
	Date Laid	Date Hatched	Sex	Ring No:	Band Color
Chick 1					
Chick2					
Chick 3					
Chick4					
Chick 5					
Chick 6					
Chick 7					
Chick 8					
Chick 9					
Chick 10					

Notes

Date Paired	Cage No:	Cock No:	Variety	Hen No:	Variety
	Date Laid	Date Hatched	Sex	Ring No:	Band Color
Chick 1					
Chick2					
Chick 3					
Chick4					
Chick 5					
Chick 6					
Chick 7					
Chick 8					
Chick 9					
Chick 10					

Notes

Date Paired	Cage No:	Cock No:	Variety	Hen No:	Variety
	Date Laid	Date Hatched	Sex	Ring No:	Band Color
Chick 1					
Chick2					
Chick 3					
Chick4					
Chick 5					
Chick 6					
Chick 7					
Chick 8					
Chick 9					
Chick 10					

Notes

Date Paired	Cage No:	Cock No:	Variety	Hen No:	Variety
	Date Laid	Date Hatched	Sex	Ring No:	Band Color
Chick 1					
Chick2					
Chick 3					
Chick4					
Chick 5					
Chick 6					
Chick 7					
Chick 8					
Chick 9					
Chick 10					

Notes

Date Paired	Cage No:	Cock No:	Variety	Hen No:	Variety
	Date Laid	Date Hatched	Sex	Ring No:	Band Color
Chick 1					
Chick2					
Chick 3					
Chick4					
Chick 5					
Chick 6					
Chick 7					
Chick 8					
Chick 9					
Chick 10					

Notes

Date Paired	Cage No:	Cock No:	Variety	Hen No:	Variety
	Date Laid	Date Hatched	Sex	Ring No:	Band Color
Chick 1					
Chick2					
Chick 3					
Chick4					
Chick 5					
Chick 6					
Chick 7					
Chick 8					
Chick 9					
Chick 10					

Notes

Date Paired	Cage No:	Cock No:	Variety	Hen No:	Variety
	Date Laid	Date Hatched	Sex	Ring No:	Band Color
Chick 1					
Chick2					
Chick 3					
Chick4					
Chick 5					
Chick 6					
Chick 7					
Chick 8					
Chick 9					
Chick 10					

Notes

Date Paired	Cage No:	Cock No:	Variety	Hen No:	Variety
	Date Laid	Date Hatched	Sex	Ring No:	Band Color
Chick 1					
Chick2					
Chick 3					
Chick4					
Chick 5					
Chick 6					
Chick 7					
Chick 8					
Chick 9					
Chick 10					

Notes

Date Paired	Cage No:	Cock No:	Variety	Hen No:	Variety
	Date Laid	Date Hatched	Sex	Ring No:	Band Color
Chick 1					
Chick2					
Chick 3					
Chick4					
Chick 5					
Chick 6					
Chick 7					
Chick 8					
Chick 9					
Chick 10					

Notes

Date Paired	Cage No:	Cock No:	Variety	Hen No:	Variety
	Date Laid	Date Hatched	Sex	Ring No:	Band Color
Chick 1					
Chick2					
Chick 3					
Chick4					
Chick 5					
Chick 6					
Chick 7					
Chick 8					
Chick 9					
Chick 10					

Notes

Date Paired	Cage No:	Cock No:	Variety	Hen No:	Variety
	Date Laid	Date Hatched	Sex	Ring No:	Band Color
Chick 1					
Chick2					
Chick 3					
Chick4					
Chick 5					
Chick 6					
Chick 7					
Chick 8					
Chick 9					
Chick 10					

Notes

Date Paired	Cage No:	Cock No:	Variety	Hen No:	Variety
	Date Laid	Date Hatched	Sex	Ring No:	Band Color
Chick 1					
Chick2					
Chick 3					
Chick4					
Chick 5					
Chick 6					
Chick 7					
Chick 8					
Chick 9					
Chick 10					

Notes

Date Paired	Cage No:	Cock No:	Variety	Hen No:	Variety
	Date Laid	Date Hatched	Sex	Ring No:	Band Color
Chick 1					
Chick2					
Chick 3					
Chick4					
Chick 5					
Chick 6					
Chick 7					
Chick 8					
Chick 9					
Chick 10					

Notes

Date Paired	Cage No:	Cock No:	Variety	Hen No:	Variety
	Date Laid	Date Hatched	Sex	Ring No:	Band Color
Chick 1					
Chick2					
Chick 3					
Chick4					
Chick 5					
Chick 6					
Chick 7					
Chick 8					
Chick 9					
Chick 10					

Notes

Date Paired	Cage No:	Cock No:	Variety	Hen No:	Variety
	Date Laid	Date Hatched	Sex	Ring No:	Band Color
Chick 1					
Chick2					
Chick 3					
Chick4					
Chick 5					
Chick 6					
Chick 7					
Chick 8					
Chick 9					
Chick 10					

Notes

Date Paired	Cage No:	Cock No:	Variety	Hen No:	Variety
	Date Laid	Date Hatched	Sex	Ring No:	Band Color
Chick 1					
Chick2					
Chick 3					
Chick4					
Chick 5					
Chick 6					
Chick 7					
Chick 8					
Chick 9					
Chick 10					

Notes

Date Paired	Cage No:	Cock No:	Variety	Hen No:	Variety
	Date Laid	Date Hatched	Sex	Ring No:	Band Color
Chick 1					
Chick2					
Chick 3					
Chick4					
Chick 5					
Chick 6					
Chick 7					
Chick 8					
Chick 9					
Chick 10					

Notes

Date Paired	Cage No:	Cock No:	Variety	Hen No:	Variety
	Date Laid	Date Hatched	Sex	Ring No:	Band Color
Chick 1					
Chick2					
Chick 3					
Chick4					
Chick 5					
Chick 6					
Chick 7					
Chick 8					
Chick 9					
Chick 10					

Notes

Date Paired	Cage No:	Cock No:	Variety	Hen No:	Variety
	Date Laid	Date Hatched	Sex	Ring No:	Band Color
Chick 1					
Chick2					
Chick 3					
Chick4					
Chick 5					
Chick 6					
Chick 7					
Chick 8					
Chick 9					
Chick 10					

Notes

Date Paired	Cage No:	Cock No:	Variety	Hen No:	Variety
	Date Laid	Date Hatched	Sex	Ring No:	Band Color
Chick 1					
Chick2					
Chick 3					
Chick4					
Chick 5					
Chick 6					
Chick 7					
Chick 8					
Chick 9					
Chick 10					

Notes

Date Paired	Cage No:	Cock No:	Variety	Hen No:	Variety
	Date Laid	Date Hatched	Sex	Ring No:	Band Color
Chick 1					
Chick2					
Chick 3					
Chick4					
Chick 5					
Chick 6					
Chick 7					
Chick 8					
Chick 9					
Chick 10					

Notes

Date Paired	Cage No:	Cock No:	Variety	Hen No:	Variety
	Date Laid	Date Hatched	Sex	Ring No:	Band Color
Chick 1					
Chick2					
Chick 3					
Chick4					
Chick 5					
Chick 6					
Chick 7					
Chick 8					
Chick 9					
Chick 10					

Notes

Date Paired	Cage No:	Cock No:	Variety	Hen No:	Variety
	Date Laid	Date Hatched	Sex	Ring No:	Band Color
Chick 1					
Chick2					
Chick 3					
Chick4					
Chick 5					
Chick 6					
Chick 7					
Chick 8					
Chick 9					
Chick 10					

Notes

Date Paired	Cage No:	Cock No:	Variety	Hen No:	Variety
	Date Laid	Date Hatched	Sex	Ring No:	Band Color
Chick 1					
Chick2					
Chick 3					
Chick4					
Chick 5					
Chick 6					
Chick 7					
Chick 8					
Chick 9					
Chick 10					

Notes

Date Paired	Cage No:	Cock No:	Variety	Hen No:	Variety
	Date Laid	Date Hatched	Sex	Ring No:	Band Color
Chick 1					
Chick2					
Chick 3					
Chick4					
Chick 5					
Chick 6					
Chick 7					
Chick 8					
Chick 9					
Chick 10					

Notes

Date Paired	Cage No:	Cock No:	Variety	Hen No:	Variety
	Date Laid	Date Hatched	Sex	Ring No:	Band Color
Chick 1					
Chick2					
Chick 3					
Chick4					
Chick 5					
Chick 6					
Chick 7					
Chick 8					
Chick 9					
Chick 10					

Notes

Date Paired	Cage No:	Cock No:	Variety	Hen No:	Variety
	Date Laid	Date Hatched	Sex	Ring No:	Band Color
Chick 1					
Chick2					
Chick 3					
Chick4					
Chick 5					
Chick 6					
Chick 7					
Chick 8					
Chick 9					
Chick 10					

Notes

Date Paired	Cage No:	Cock No:	Variety	Hen No:	Variety
	Date Laid	Date Hatched	Sex	Ring No:	Band Color
Chick 1					
Chick2					
Chick 3					
Chick4					
Chick 5					
Chick 6					
Chick 7					
Chick 8					
Chick 9					
Chick 10					

Notes

Date Paired	Cage No:	Cock No:	Variety	Hen No:	Variety
	Date Laid	Date Hatched	Sex	Ring No:	Band Color
Chick 1					
Chick2					
Chick 3					
Chick4					
Chick 5					
Chick 6					
Chick 7					
Chick 8					
Chick 9					
Chick 10					

Notes

Date Paired	Cage No:	Cock No:	Variety	Hen No:	Variety
	Date Laid	Date Hatched	Sex	Ring No:	Band Color
Chick 1					
Chick2					
Chick 3					
Chick4					
Chick 5					
Chick 6					
Chick 7					
Chick 8					
Chick 9					
Chick 10					

Notes

Date Paired	Cage No:	Cock No:	Variety	Hen No:	Variety
	Date Laid	Date Hatched	Sex	Ring No:	Band Color
Chick 1					
Chick2					
Chick 3					
Chick4					
Chick 5					
Chick 6					
Chick 7					
Chick 8					
Chick 9					
Chick 10					

Notes

Date Paired	Cage No:	Cock No:	Variety	Hen No:	Variety
	Date Laid	Date Hatched	Sex	Ring No:	Band Color
Chick 1					
Chick2					
Chick 3					
Chick4					
Chick 5					
Chick 6					
Chick 7					
Chick 8					
Chick 9					
Chick 10					

Notes

Date Paired	Cage No:	Cock No:	Variety	Hen No:	Variety
	Date Laid	Date Hatched	Sex	Ring No:	Band Color
Chick 1					
Chick2					
Chick 3					
Chick4					
Chick 5					
Chick 6					
Chick 7					
Chick 8					
Chick 9					
Chick 10					

Notes

Date Paired	Cage No:	Cock No:	Variety	Hen No:	Variety
	Date Laid	Date Hatched	Sex	Ring No:	Band Color
Chick 1					
Chick2					
Chick 3					
Chick4					
Chick 5					
Chick 6					
Chick 7					
Chick 8					
Chick 9					
Chick 10					

Notes

Date Paired	Cage No:	Cock No:	Variety	Hen No:	Variety
	Date Laid	Date Hatched	Sex	Ring No:	Band Color
Chick 1					
Chick2					
Chick 3					
Chick4					
Chick 5					
Chick 6					
Chick 7					
Chick 8					
Chick 9					
Chick 10					

Notes

Date Paired	Cage No:	Cock No:	Variety	Hen No:	Variety
	Date Laid	Date Hatched	Sex	Ring No:	Band Color
Chick 1					
Chick2					
Chick 3					
Chick4					
Chick 5					
Chick 6					
Chick 7					
Chick 8					
Chick 9					
Chick 10					

Notes

Date Paired	Cage No:	Cock No:	Variety	Hen No:	Variety
	Date Laid	Date Hatched	Sex	Ring No:	Band Color
Chick 1					
Chick2					
Chick 3					
Chick4					
Chick 5					
Chick 6					
Chick 7					
Chick 8					
Chick 9					
Chick 10					

Notes

Date Paired	Cage No:	Cock No:	Variety	Hen No:	Variety
	Date Laid	Date Hatched	Sex	Ring No:	Band Color
Chick 1					
Chick2					
Chick 3					
Chick4					
Chick 5					
Chick 6					
Chick 7					
Chick 8					
Chick 9					
Chick 10					

Notes

Date Paired	Cage No:	Cock No:	Variety	Hen No:	Variety
	Date Laid	Date Hatched	Sex	Ring No:	Band Color
Chick 1					
Chick2					
Chick 3					
Chick4					
Chick 5					
Chick 6					
Chick 7					
Chick 8					
Chick 9					
Chick 10					

Notes

Date Paired	Cage No:	Cock No:	Variety	Hen No:	Variety
	Date Laid	Date Hatched	Sex	Ring No:	Band Color
Chick 1					
Chick2					
Chick 3					
Chick4					
Chick 5					
Chick 6					
Chick 7					
Chick 8					
Chick 9					
Chick 10					

Notes

Date Paired	Cage No:	Cock No:	Variety	Hen No:	Variety
	Date Laid	Date Hatched	Sex	Ring No:	Band Color
Chick 1					
Chick2					
Chick 3					
Chick4					
Chick 5					
Chick 6					
Chick 7					
Chick 8					
Chick 9					
Chick 10					

Notes

Date Paired	Cage No:	Cock No:	Variety	Hen No:	Variety
	Date Laid	Date Hatched	Sex	Ring No:	Band Color
Chick 1					
Chick2					
Chick 3					
Chick4					
Chick 5					
Chick 6					
Chick 7					
Chick 8					
Chick 9					
Chick 10					

Notes

Date Paired	Cage No:	Cock No:	Variety	Hen No:	Variety
	Date Laid	Date Hatched	Sex	Ring No:	Band Color
Chick 1					
Chick2					
Chick 3					
Chick4					
Chick 5					
Chick 6					
Chick 7					
Chick 8					
Chick 9					
Chick 10					

Notes

Date Paired	Cage No:	Cock No:	Variety	Hen No:	Variety
	Date Laid	Date Hatched	Sex	Ring No:	Band Color
Chick 1					
Chick2					
Chick 3					
Chick4					
Chick 5					
Chick 6					
Chick 7					
Chick 8					
Chick 9					
Chick 10					

Notes

Date Paired	Cage No:	Cock No:	Variety	Hen No:	Variety
	Date Laid	Date Hatched	Sex	Ring No:	Band Color
Chick 1					
Chick2					
Chick 3					
Chick4					
Chick 5					
Chick 6					
Chick 7					
Chick 8					
Chick 9					
Chick 10					

Notes

Date Paired	Cage No:	Cock No:	Variety	Hen No:	Variety
	Date Laid	Date Hatched	Sex	Ring No:	Band Color
Chick 1					
Chick2					
Chick 3					
Chick4					
Chick 5					
Chick 6					
Chick 7					
Chick 8					
Chick 9					
Chick 10					

Notes

Date Paired	Cage No:	Cock No:	Variety	Hen No:	Variety
	Date Laid	Date Hatched	Sex	Ring No:	Band Color
Chick 1					
Chick2					
Chick 3					
Chick4					
Chick 5					
Chick 6					
Chick 7					
Chick 8					
Chick 9					
Chick 10					

Notes

Date Paired	Cage No:	Cock No:	Variety	Hen No:	Variety
	Date Laid	Date Hatched	Sex	Ring No:	Band Color
Chick 1					
Chick2					
Chick 3					
Chick4					
Chick 5					
Chick 6					
Chick 7					
Chick 8					
Chick 9					
Chick 10					

Notes

Date Paired	Cage No:	Cock No:	Variety	Hen No:	Variety
	Date Laid	Date Hatched	Sex	Ring No:	Band Color
Chick 1					
Chick2					
Chick 3					
Chick4					
Chick 5					
Chick 6					
Chick 7					
Chick 8					
Chick 9					
Chick 10					

Notes

Date Paired	Cage No:	Cock No:	Variety	Hen No:	Variety
	Date Laid	Date Hatched	Sex	Ring No:	Band Color
Chick 1					
Chick2					
Chick 3					
Chick4					
Chick 5					
Chick 6					
Chick 7					
Chick 8					
Chick 9					
Chick 10					

Notes

Date Paired	Cage No:	Cock No:	Variety	Hen No:	Variety
	Date Laid	Date Hatched	Sex	Ring No:	Band Color
Chick 1					
Chick2					
Chick 3					
Chick4					
Chick 5					
Chick 6					
Chick 7					
Chick 8					
Chick 9					
Chick 10					

Notes

Date Paired	Cage No:	Cock No:	Variety	Hen No:	Variety
	Date Laid	Date Hatched	Sex	Ring No:	Band Color
Chick 1					
Chick2					
Chick 3					
Chick4					
Chick 5					
Chick 6					
Chick 7					
Chick 8					
Chick 9					
Chick 10					

Notes

Date Paired	Cage No:	Cock No:	Variety	Hen No:	Variety
	Date Laid	Date Hatched	Sex	Ring No:	Band Color
Chick 1					
Chick2					
Chick 3					
Chick4					
Chick 5					
Chick 6					
Chick 7					
Chick 8					
Chick 9					
Chick 10					

Notes

Date Paired	Cage No:	Cock No:	Variety	Hen No:	Variety
	Date Laid	Date Hatched	Sex	Ring No:	Band Color
Chick 1					
Chick2					
Chick 3					
Chick4					
Chick 5					
Chick 6					
Chick 7					
Chick 8					
Chick 9					
Chick 10					

Notes

Date Paired	Cage No:	Cock No:	Variety	Hen No:	Variety
	Date Laid	Date Hatched	Sex	Ring No:	Band Color
Chick 1					
Chick2					
Chick 3					
Chick4					
Chick 5					
Chick 6					
Chick 7					
Chick 8					
Chick 9					
Chick 10					

Notes

Date Paired	Cage No:	Cock No:	Variety	Hen No:	Variety
	Date Laid	Date Hatched	Sex	Ring No:	Band Color
Chick 1					
Chick2					
Chick 3					
Chick4					
Chick 5					
Chick 6					
Chick 7					
Chick 8					
Chick 9					
Chick 10					

Notes

Date Paired	Cage No:	Cock No:	Variety	Hen No:	Variety
	Date Laid	Date Hatched	Sex	Ring No:	Band Color
Chick 1					
Chick2					
Chick 3					
Chick4					
Chick 5					
Chick 6					
Chick 7					
Chick 8					
Chick 9					
Chick 10					

Notes

Date Paired	Cage No:	Cock No:	Variety	Hen No:	Variety
	Date Laid	Date Hatched	Sex	Ring No:	Band Color
Chick 1					
Chick2					
Chick 3					
Chick4					
Chick 5					
Chick 6					
Chick 7					
Chick 8					
Chick 9					
Chick 10					

Notes

Date Paired	Cage No:	Cock No:	Variety	Hen No:	Variety
	Date Laid	Date Hatched	Sex	Ring No:	Band Color
Chick 1					
Chick2					
Chick 3					
Chick4					
Chick 5					
Chick 6					
Chick 7					
Chick 8					
Chick 9					
Chick 10					

Notes

Date Paired	Cage No:	Cock No:	Variety	Hen No:	Variety
	Date Laid	Date Hatched	Sex	Ring No:	Band Color
Chick 1					
Chick2					
Chick 3					
Chick4					
Chick 5					
Chick 6					
Chick 7					
Chick 8					
Chick 9					
Chick 10					

Notes

Date Paired	Cage No:	Cock No:	Variety	Hen No:	Variety
	Date Laid	Date Hatched	Sex	Ring No:	Band Color
Chick 1					
Chick2					
Chick 3					
Chick4					
Chick 5					
Chick 6					
Chick 7					
Chick 8					
Chick 9					
Chick 10					

Notes

Date Paired	Cage No:	Cock No:	Variety	Hen No:	Variety
	Date Laid	Date Hatched	Sex	Ring No:	Band Color
Chick 1					
Chick2					
Chick 3					
Chick4					
Chick 5					
Chick 6					
Chick 7					
Chick 8					
Chick 9					
Chick 10					

Notes

Date Paired	Cage No:	Cock No:	Variety	Hen No:	Variety
	Date Laid	Date Hatched	Sex	Ring No:	Band Color
Chick 1					
Chick2					
Chick 3					
Chick4					
Chick 5					
Chick 6					
Chick 7					
Chick 8					
Chick 9					
Chick 10					

Notes

Date Paired	Cage No:	Cock No:	Variety	Hen No:	Variety
	Date Laid	Date Hatched	Sex	Ring No:	Band Color
Chick 1					
Chick2					
Chick 3					
Chick4					
Chick 5					
Chick 6					
Chick 7					
Chick 8					
Chick 9					
Chick 10					

Notes

Date Paired	Cage No:	Cock No:	Variety	Hen No:	Variety
	Date Laid	Date Hatched	Sex	Ring No:	Band Color
Chick 1					
Chick2					
Chick 3					
Chick4					
Chick 5					
Chick 6					
Chick 7					
Chick 8					
Chick 9					
Chick 10					

Notes

Date Paired	Cage No:	Cock No:	Variety	Hen No:	Variety
	Date Laid	Date Hatched	Sex	Ring No:	Band Color
Chick 1					
Chick2					
Chick 3					
Chick4					
Chick 5					
Chick 6					
Chick 7					
Chick 8					
Chick 9					
Chick 10					

Notes

Date Paired	Cage No:	Cock No:	Variety	Hen No:	Variety
	Date Laid	Date Hatched	Sex	Ring No:	Band Color
Chick 1					
Chick2					
Chick 3					
Chick4					
Chick 5					
Chick 6					
Chick 7					
Chick 8					
Chick 9					
Chick 10					

Notes

Date Paired	Cage No:	Cock No:	Variety	Hen No:	Variety
	Date Laid	Date Hatched	Sex	Ring No:	Band Color
Chick 1					
Chick2					
Chick 3					
Chick4					
Chick 5					
Chick 6					
Chick 7					
Chick 8					
Chick 9					
Chick 10					

Notes

Date Paired	Cage No:	Cock No:	Variety	Hen No:	Variety
	Date Laid	Date Hatched	Sex	Ring No:	Band Color
Chick 1					
Chick2					
Chick 3					
Chick4					
Chick 5					
Chick 6					
Chick 7					
Chick 8					
Chick 9					
Chick 10					

Notes

Date Paired	Cage No:	Cock No:	Variety	Hen No:	Variety
	Date Laid	Date Hatched	Sex	Ring No:	Band Color
Chick 1					
Chick2					
Chick 3					
Chick4					
Chick 5					
Chick 6					
Chick 7					
Chick 8					
Chick 9					
Chick 10					

Notes

Date Paired	Cage No:	Cock No:	Variety	Hen No:	Variety
	Date Laid	Date Hatched	Sex	Ring No:	Band Color
Chick 1					
Chick2					
Chick 3					
Chick4					
Chick 5					
Chick 6					
Chick 7					
Chick 8					
Chick 9					
Chick 10					

Notes

Date Paired	Cage No:	Cock No:	Variety	Hen No:	Variety
	Date Laid	Date Hatched	Sex	Ring No:	Band Color
Chick 1					
Chick2					
Chick 3					
Chick4					
Chick 5					
Chick 6					
Chick 7					
Chick 8					
Chick 9					
Chick 10					

Notes

Date Paired	Cage No:	Cock No:	Variety	Hen No:	Variety
	Date Laid	Date Hatched	Sex	Ring No:	Band Color
Chick 1					
Chick2					
Chick 3					
Chick4					
Chick 5					
Chick 6					
Chick 7					
Chick 8					
Chick 9					
Chick 10					

Notes

Date Paired	Cage No:	Cock No:	Variety	Hen No:	Variety
	Date Laid	Date Hatched	Sex	Ring No:	Band Color
Chick 1					
Chick2					
Chick 3					
Chick4					
Chick 5					
Chick 6					
Chick 7					
Chick 8					
Chick 9					
Chick 10					

Notes

Date Paired	Cage No:	Cock No:	Variety	Hen No:	Variety
	Date Laid	Date Hatched	Sex	Ring No:	Band Color
Chick 1					
Chick2					
Chick 3					
Chick4					
Chick 5					
Chick 6					
Chick 7					
Chick 8					
Chick 9					
Chick 10					

Notes

Date Paired	Cage No:	Cock No:	Variety	Hen No:	Variety
	Date Laid	Date Hatched	Sex	Ring No:	Band Color
Chick 1					
Chick2					
Chick 3					
Chick4					
Chick 5					
Chick 6					
Chick 7					
Chick 8					
Chick 9					
Chick 10					

Notes

Date Paired	Cage No:	Cock No:	Variety	Hen No:	Variety
	Date Laid	Date Hatched	Sex	Ring No:	Band Color
Chick 1					
Chick2					
Chick 3					
Chick4					
Chick 5					
Chick 6					
Chick 7					
Chick 8					
Chick 9					
Chick 10					

Notes

Date Paired	Cage No:	Cock No:	Variety	Hen No:	Variety
	Date Laid	Date Hatched	Sex	Ring No:	Band Color
Chick 1					
Chick2					
Chick 3					
Chick4					
Chick 5					
Chick 6					
Chick 7					
Chick 8					
Chick 9					
Chick 10					

Notes

Date Paired	Cage No:	Cock No:	Variety	Hen No:	Variety
	Date Laid	Date Hatched	Sex	Ring No:	Band Color
Chick 1					
Chick2					
Chick 3					
Chick4					
Chick 5					
Chick 6					
Chick 7					
Chick 8					
Chick 9					
Chick 10					

Notes

Date Paired	Cage No:	Cock No:	Variety	Hen No:	Variety
	Date Laid	Date Hatched	Sex	Ring No:	Band Color
Chick 1					
Chick2					
Chick 3					
Chick4					
Chick 5					
Chick 6					
Chick 7					
Chick 8					
Chick 9					
Chick 10					

Notes

Date Paired	Cage No:	Cock No:	Variety	Hen No:	Variety
	Date Laid	Date Hatched	Sex	Ring No:	Band Color
Chick 1					
Chick2					
Chick 3					
Chick4					
Chick 5					
Chick 6					
Chick 7					
Chick 8					
Chick 9					
Chick 10					

Notes

Date Paired	Cage No:	Cock No:	Variety	Hen No:	Variety
	Date Laid	Date Hatched	Sex	Ring No:	Band Color
Chick 1					
Chick2					
Chick 3					
Chick4					
Chick 5					
Chick 6					
Chick 7					
Chick 8					
Chick 9					
Chick 10					

Notes

Date Paired	Cage No:	Cock No:	Variety	Hen No:	Variety
	Date Laid	Date Hatched	Sex	Ring No:	Band Color
Chick 1					
Chick2					
Chick 3					
Chick4					
Chick 5					
Chick 6					
Chick 7					
Chick 8					
Chick 9					
Chick 10					

Notes

Date Paired	Cage No:	Cock No:	Variety	Hen No:	Variety
	Date Laid	Date Hatched	Sex	Ring No:	Band Color
Chick 1					
Chick2					
Chick 3					
Chick4					
Chick 5					
Chick 6					
Chick 7					
Chick 8					
Chick 9					
Chick 10					

Notes

Made in the USA
Las Vegas, NV
02 February 2022

42899560R00057